I'm a FEEL -O- SAUR

by Lezlie Evans

illustrated by Kate Chappell

WELBECK

Emotions are inside us all.
Some are big and some are small.
These dino-kids are just like you—
at times they're brave;
sometimes they're blue.

let's meet the dinos one-by-one
and have some feel-o-saurus fun!

Happy-saurus wears a smile
that shows his big teeth for a mile.
He jumps and skips
and loves to prance.
He often does a dino-dance.

When Happy-saurus comes your way
it's sure to be a brilliant day!

When **Shy-o-saurus** comes around, he rarely ever makes a sound.

Big crowds of dinos make him **sweat**.

School plays cause him to **fret**.

For him, it's really not absurd
to **play alone**, far from the herd.

But when you get
him one-on-one,

this dino-kid is **super fun!**

Meet **Angry-saurus**.
In she bounds—
her stomp, stomp, stomping
shakes the ground.

She slaps her tail
and claws the air.
She gives the meanest,
awful glare.

She huffs and puffs,
she gulps and gasps.
"I'm so upset,"
she roars and rasps.

This dino needs to
count to ten,

take two **deep breaths** ...
and **start again.**

When things **go wrong**
throughout his day,

when big sis says,
"You **cannot** play,"

this **Sad-o-saurus**
gives a pout,

then lets his **dino-feelings** out.

There is one thing that's sure to ease
his gloomy mood ...

a **loving** squeeze.

When **Silly-saurus**
gets the giggles,
she can't **stop**,
her bottom **wiggles**.

She puts her clothes on
inside out,

then cries,

"Whoop-whoop!"

and struts about.

She makes the other dinos

roarrr

and roll with laughter on the floor.

When **Scared-o-saurus**
starts to shake,
she feels her long legs
quiver, quake.

Her stomach twists,
her eyes grow wide,
and this big dino
tries to **hide.**

Some things are SCARY, at first glance.
But if she gives them half a chance

and breathes in deep, counts 1-2-3 ...
when she breathes out, her jitters flee!

Excite-o-saurus

cannot wait!
Today she's got a fun play date.

Her tummy flits,
  her feet tap, tap.

Her eyes grow wide,
  her wings go flap.

She finds that she
is **all aglow**
when Mama-saurus says,
"Let's go!"

She jumps around
and shouts,
"Hooray!

"I'm going to have the best-est day!"

Bored-o-saurus wears a frown.

He moans and groans and **mopes around.**

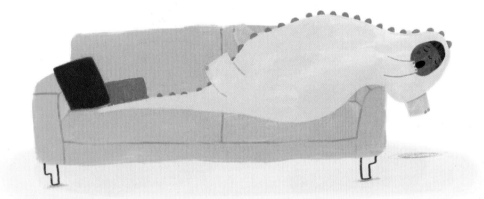

When he can't think of things to do,

this guy is prone to **fuss** and **stew**.

Of all the dinos,
he's the one
that needs to get out in the sun

to kick a ball,
go for a run,
and find some friends
to **join the fun.**

The **Grumpy-saurus**
might look cute
in his little dino suit,

but then ... a whimper,
whine,

and
SNAP!

You know he's tired
and needs a **nap.**

Another reason for his mood:
his rumbling tummy needs some
FOOD!

When he eats and
gets his rest,
Grumpy-saurus is
the **best!**

Brave-o-saurus

stands her ground.

If there's a challenge
she'll be found
with head held **high**
and wings spread **wide**-
sheer grit and purpose as her guide.

She may be scared,
but soon she'll fly

'cause this **brave** dino
dares to **try**.

Do a dino-dance!

HAPPY-SAURUS

Ask a parent or friend for a hug.

SAD-O-SAURUS

Feelings change
throughout the day,
Some **up**, some **down**—
and that's **okay!**
So many moods we all go through ...

What kind of FEEL-O-SAUR are you?

When feeling silly, sad or shy,
give these dino-tips a try.

Take two deep breaths and count to 10.

ANGRY-SAURUS

Invite a friend to have a play date.

EXCITE-O-SAURUS

Make up funny words to one of your favorite songs.

Try smiling at a new friend.

SILLY-SAURUS

Draw a picture of yourself defeating your fear.

SHY-O-SAURUS

SCARED-O-SAURUS

Make a list of fun things to do. Try something new!

Do something nice for somebody else.

Stand up for someone who is being teased or bullied.

BORED-O-SAURUS

GRUMPY-SAURUS

BRAVE-O-SAURUS

For my grandchildren, who make me
feel like a Joy-o-saurus! – L.E.

For Bella, for always being
our Happy-saurus. – K.C.

First published in Great Britain in 2021 by Welbeck Children's Books
An imprint of Welbeck Children's Limited, part of the Welbeck Publishing Group.
20 Mortimer Street, London W1T 3JW.

This edition published in the United States in 2021 by Welbeck Children's Books
An imprint of Welbeck Children's Limited, part of the Welbeck Publishing Group.

ISBN: 978-1-78312-709-2

10 9 8 7 6 5 4 3 2 1

Designed by Kathryn Davies
Printed and bound in Dongguan, China
Paper from responsible sources

It is imperative to a child's wellbeing to teach him or her about all of the emotions, allow them to feel and express them, and give them the tools to manage these feelings. *I'm a Feel-o-saur* encourages children to explore different emotional states in a fun and safe way. This picture book is relatable and entertaining, and it helps to normalise the experience of both positive and negative feelings. It has been handpicked by our specialist team at Upside Down Books to introduce children to a wide-ranging emotional vocabulary. Read this with your children to find out how they are feeling, and you might just identify with one of the feel-o-saurs yourself!

Lauren Callaghan

Consultant Clinical Psychologist,
Co-founder and Clinical Director of Trigger Publishing